The First Continental Congress

A Short History

Doug West, Ph.D

C&D Publications

The First Continental Congress

A Short History

By Doug West, Ph.D.

ISBN: 9798521742929

Table of Contents

Preface

Welcome to the book, *The First Continental Congress, A Short History*. This book is volume 55 of the 30 Minute Book Series, and as the name of the series implies, if you are an average reader this book should take less than an hour to read. Since this short book is not meant to be an all-encompassing history of the First Continental Congress, you may want to know more about this pivotal moment in American history. To help you with this, there are several good references at the end of this book. I have also provided a Timeline, in order to link together the important events of the Congress, and a section of the book titled "Biographical Sketches," which includes brief biographies of some of the key individuals in the book. In the text, those individuals who are in one of the biographical sketches will have their name in **bold** print the first time they appear in the book.

Thank you for purchasing this book. I hope you enjoy your time reading about the First Continental Congress of the United States.

Doug West

June 2021

DOUG WEST, PH.D.

Introduction

Following the lead of the Spaniards, in 1607 the British established a foothold in North America with a fledgling colony in Jamestown in Virginia. For the next 150 years, English men and women immigrated to America, the new land of opportunity, seeking to build a better life. Along with the English came French, more Spanish, and Dutch colonists hoping to expand their domains into this new frontier. Friction arose between the two arch-rivals, Great Britain and France, over trade and land rights in America, culminating in 1754 with the start of the French and Indian War. Though the English ultimately defeated the French, nearly driving them out of North America, the near decade long war left Britain deeply in debt. British statesmen believed that the colonies in America ought to bear a greater portion of the cost of administering and defending the colonies and began to impose new taxes. Here is where the troubles began between the British colonists living in America and the mother country.

Britain, desperate to rebuild their treasury and fund the large contingency of British troops stationed in America, started to enact a series of taxes upon the colonists. Facing protests in the colonies, in 1770, the British Prime Minister Lord North repealed the recently introduced taxes on commodities, with one exception, the duty on tea. The new taxes were extremely unpopular in the colonies as they felt that Parliament had no right to tax them since they had no representation in Parliament. Lord North proclaimed Parliament's authority, "as a mark of the supremacy of Parliament, and an efficient declaration of their right to govern the colonies." Many Americans were coming to grips with the reality that their rights and their liberties were being threatened by British power. In Boston, angry colonists organized and protested under the leadership of the radical **Samuel Adams**. By late 1773, independence was being openly discussed in colonial newspapers. As the British Crown under **King George III** and the Parliament under Lord North stiffened their resolve to control the American colonies, a confrontation between the British government and the rebels seemed to be an inevitability.

As the embers of revolution smoldered, all that was required to set the flame was a spark, which came in the form of the Tea Act of 1773. This law was designed to keep the financially troubled East India Company from going into bankruptcy. Parliament threw the beleaguered company a lifeline in the form of granting them a monopoly on the sale of tea to the English colonies in America. What seemed like a straightforward act of government to rescue a major British company set off a series of events that brought delegates from 12 of the 13 colonies in America together in Philadelphia to form the First Continental Congress. The 56 delegates came together with the purpose of seeking redress for their grievances against their mother country.

This is the story of how a small group of men with quite different backgrounds worked diligently to lay the cornerstone of the foundation of a new nation.

Chapter 1 -
Growing Unrest in the American Colonies Over the Tea Act

"The revolution was effected before the war commenced. The revolution was in the minds and hearts of the people." – John Adams

Unrest stirred in the towns and cities that dotted the eastern seaboard of colonial America when the citizens learned that Parliament had enacted the Tea Act in May 1773. This act gave the London based East India Company a monopoly on the sale of tea in the British colonies of North America. The East India Company was a major British company trading in commodities from the Far East and was in financial trouble. It held large stockpiles of tea stored in London warehouses that it could not sell. To bail out the company, Parliament passed the Tea Act to allow the company to dump its surplus tea on the American colonial market. In the colonies, most tea sold was smuggled in from Holland. The smuggled "Dutch Tea" was cheaper than the British tea since it was effectively duty free. Even though the tea from the East India Company was less expensive to the tea drinkers, the American tea merchants, both legal and the smugglers, would be seriously hurt by the cheap tea.

With so many colonial merchants involved in the distribution and sale of tea, the new law potentially had significant consequences for their businesses. To add further upset to the colonists, built into the price of the tea was a small tax that went back to the British government. In September 1773, seven ships laden with tea from the East India Company set sail for the port cities of Boston, New York, Philadelphia, and Charleston.

On October 21, 1773, the Massachusetts Committee of Correspondence sent a letter signed by Samuel Adams and Thomas Cushing to the other colonies urging them to "be united" in rejecting the tea bound for America. Adams, making a call for colonial unity, wrote in the *Boston Gazette* under the pen name "Observation" proposing "a congress of American States be assembled as soon as possible; draw up a Bill of Rights; …choose an ambassador to reside at the British court to act for the united colonies; appoint where the congress shall annually meet."

The *Dartmouth* arrived in Boston Harbor on Sunday, November 28, loaded with the hated tea. According to customs rules, within 20 days duties on the tea must be paid and the cargo unloaded, or it would be impounded and sold for the unpaid duties. Two more ships arrived a few days after the *Dartmouth*, also loaded with tea. Thomas Hutchinson, the British loyalist governor of Massachusetts, ordered that the three ships be unloaded over the loud objections of the colonists. The radical group, the Sons of Liberty, of which Adams was one of the ringleaders, declared that anyone who aided in unloading or selling the British tea when it arrived would be considered as one of the "enemies of America."

The Boston Tea Party

December 17 was the day when the 20 days were up, and the tea had to be unloaded per the order of the governor. Anger was growing within the ranks of the patriots over the tea remaining in the port. On the night of December 16, the colonists decided to take matters into their own hands. Samuel Adams and fellow patriots held a large rally at Boston's Old South Church to decide what to do about the tea. When the meeting disbanded, a group of around 160 men dressed as Mohawk Indians marched to Griffin's Wharf, boarded the three ships, and without damaging the ships or assaulting the crew, proceeded to throw overboard over three hundred chests of tea into Massachusetts Bay. The next day, Samuel Adams set to work writing letters to the other colonies informing them of the happenings in Boston. "This is the most magnificent movement of all," exulted Samuel's cousin, the lawyer **John Adams**, adding, "This destruction of the tea is so bold, so daring, so firm, intrepid, and inflexible, and it must have so important consequences, and so lasting, that I can't but consider it an epoch in history." The British authorities were outraged with the episode, valuing the tea at a hefty £10,000 sterling. In Philadelphia and New York, the tea-laden ships were rejected by the colonists and forced to return to England with their cargo. In Charleston, the tea was unloaded and placed in a cellar where it remained until 1776.

Figure – The Boston Tea Party.

The Coercive Acts

As soon as word reached England of the "Boston Tea Party," Parliament's retaliation was swift and decisive. Parliament issued a set of punitive laws they collectively called the "Coercive Acts," which the colonists called the "Intolerable Acts." The most economically crippling of the acts was the Boston Port Act, which closed the harbor starting June 1, 1774, until the city paid for the destroyed tea. The Act for the Impartial Administration of Justice let the royal governor transfer to England the trial of any British official accused of committing a capital offense in the line of duty, effectively making the British immune from colonial justice for serious crimes.

The Quartering Act required local authorities to provide lodging for British soldiers, in private homes if necessary. Lastly, the Massachusetts Government Act virtually annulled the colony's 1691 charter and gave the royal governor control over town meetings. In May, the civilian governor Hutchinson was replaced by General Thomas Gage, putting Boston under military control with 4,000 British troops, called "redcoats" by the colonists, stationed in the city for enforcement. The British assumed the Coercive Acts would bring the colonists to heal; instead, it galvanized their resistance. Sympathetic colonists up and down the eastern seaboard rallied to the cause of the besieged Bostonians, sending money, provisions, and boycotting British goods.

Resistance Grows Throughout the Colonies

Rumors of the British blockade of the Boston port had been circulating in Williamsburg, Virginia, for days. Two weeks into the Virginia General Assembly session, the *Virginia Gazette* ran an article outlining the desperate state in Boston. Thomas Jefferson, Patrick Henry, Richard Henry Lee, and a handful of the younger burgesses became alarmed, believing something must be done to alert Virginians of the British aggression. On May 23, they called a secret meeting and introduced a resolution calling for "a day of fasting, humiliation, and prayer" to occur on June 1, the day the port of Boston was to be closed. Their purpose was to dramatize to the people the eminent danger inherent in the British actions in Boston. The governor of Virginia immediately dissolved the House of Burgesses, forcing the members to meet in private at Raleigh Tavern. The burgesses denounced the closure of the Boston Harbor as "a most dangerous attempt to destroy the constitutional liberty and rights of all North America," declaring that an attack upon one colony was an attack upon all. They called for a general congress of deputies from all of the colonies to meet and deliberate on such measures as "the united interests of America from time to time required." In mid-June, the Massachusetts House of Representatives resolved "that a meeting of Committees, from the several Colonies on the Continent is highly expedient and necessary, to consult upon the present state of the Colonies." They recommended that a meeting of representatives from all of the colonies convene in Philadelphia on September 1. Elsewhere, to coordinate the colonial response to the crisis, proposals came out of town meetings in Providence, Rhode Island, and the committees of correspondence in Philadelphia and New York for a general meeting of all the colonies. As word spread of the planned meeting, all the colonies except Georgia began the process of selecting delegates for the upcoming Congress.

Even with the harsh treatment by the Parliament, most of the English living in the American colonies were loyal to the British Crown and had no desire to separate from their mother country. As the revolutionary writer **John Dickinson** put it in his popular set of essays, *Letters from a Farmer in Pennsylvania*, most English in America were bound to the Crown "by religion, liberty, laws, affections, relations, language, and commerce." Some supported the actions of the British, feeling the willful destruction of the tea was an illegal act requiring a reckoning, while most hoped the crisis would just go away so they could get on with their daily lives. Many in the colonies were surely unaware of the extent of the British aggression in New England; only the major newspapers in the largest of cities had significant circulation to spread the news deep into the hinterland, thus leaving many unaware of the distress of Boston.

Chapter 2 – Setting the Stage for the First Continental Congress

"The distinctions between Virginians, Pennsylvanians, New Yorkers, and New Englanders are no more. I am not a Virginian but an American." – Patrick Henry.

The people of Philadelphia warmly welcomed the delegates to the First Continental Congress as they arrived in the city. The delegates were from 12 of the 13 colonies; only Georgia did not send any representatives due to its strong loyalist leanings. For most of the delegates this was their first time traveling such a great distance from home. Many traveled for weeks to get to the city of brotherly love. Philadelphia, with 38,000 inhabitants, was by far the largest city in Colonial America. New York City, with a population of 22,000, and Boston, with 17,000 people, were a distant second and third. Situated on the neck of land about two miles wide between the Delaware and Schuylkill rivers, Philadelphia was America's busiest port, with wharfs stretching nearly two miles along the Delaware River. Ships out bound from the city carried lumber and wheat, Pennsylvania's chief exports. Ships from Europe and the West Indies brought finished goods, sugar, molasses, spices, and gunpowder. Philadelphia was unusual in that it had been a planned city, rather than just unfolding like most colonial cities. One of the delegates, John Adams, as he explored his new temporary home recorded the layout of the city in his journal: "Front Street is near the river, then 2nd Street, 3rd, 4th, 5th, 6th, 7th, 8th, 9th. The cross streets which intersect these are all equally wide, straight and parallel to each other, and are named for forest and fruit trees, Pear Street, Apple Street, Walnut Street, Chestnut Street, etc."

The Delegates

56 delegates in all were chosen to attend the convention by the assemblies of each of the colonies. The distinguished group consisted mainly of middle-aged property owners, with several being very wealthy. Many of the men were well educated, with degrees from European universities as well as Harvard, Yale, William and Mary College, and other colonial schools. Nineteen future signers of a document yet to be written, the Declaration of Independence, were among the group, as well as two future presidents. The small group of men represented some of the best and brightest minds the colonial assemblies had to offer the Congress.

Samuel Adams, one of the Massachusetts delegates, was known for his radical stance and unlike the other delegates was not wealthy or in a position of power. He had failed as a brewer and was the clerk of the Massachusetts Assembly. The last many years of his life were spent fostering the revolutionary cause and thinking little of building his own personal fortune. **Joseph Galloway**, a prosperous and polished Philadelphia lawyer who aspired to the leadership of the conservatives in Congress, summed up Samuel Adams as such: "A man, who though by no means remarkable for brilliant abilities, yet is equal to most men in popular intrigue, and the management of a faction. He eats little, drinks little, sleeps little, thinks much, and is most indefatigable in the pursuit of his objectives." Samuel's cousin, the lawyer John Adams, was also a Massachusetts delegate to the Congress. John, though lacking Samuel's fervor, was an ardent American patriot. Short and stout, with a bit of a paunch, John Adams loved to record the day's events in his diary. His diary, which he kept off and on for 50 years, has given historians insight into daily life in Colonial America and the important events that defined the Revolutionary Era. His prolific writings throughout the revolutionary period have been an invaluable source of firsthand accounts of some of the turning points in the formation of the United States.

The Massachusetts delegation consisted of John Adams, Samuel Adams, and the two successful lawyers, Thomas Cushing and Thomas Treat Paine. According to John Adams' accounting of the journey, the men traveled in Cushing's handsome carriage along with six servants. When they left on August 10, 1774, New England was still hot and dry, transforming the compact highway into a choking, dusty thoroughfare. From Boston, the men traveled through Connecticut, New York, New Jersey, and finally arrived in Philadelphia on August 29. Along the journey, as they passed through the towns and villages the men were greeted and welcomed by the local officials and the citizens. The delegates listened closely to gain the sentiments of the common man. Were they hardened revolutionaries? British loyalists? Or somewhere in between? In Hartford, Connecticut, they met with a delegate from Connecticut, Silas Deane, who declared, "The Congress is the grandest and most important assembly ever held in America…All of America is entrusted to it and depends upon it."

In Philadelphia, one of the delegates from Delaware, Caesar Rodney, caught Adams' attention. He wrote: "[Rodney] is the oddest looking man in the world; he is tall, thin and slender as a reed, pale; his face is not bigger than a large apple, yet there is sense and fire, spirit, wit, and humor in his countenance." Rodney wrote of his fellow delegates, "All the seven delegates appointed for Virginia are here and more sensible fine fellows you'd never wish to see, in short it is the greatest assembly that ever was collected in America." Rodney went on to say many had condemned the Bostonians for their violence, but when he compared them to the men from Virginia, South Carolina, and Rhode Island, they were moderate men. Perhaps the South Carolina delegate Christopher Gadsden was the fieriest for liberty. Silas Deane wrote of Gadsden, "Mr. Gadsden leaves all New England Sons of Liberty far behind, for he is for taking up his firelock and marching direct to Boston." Gadsden confirmed that "were his wife and children all in Boston, and they were to perish by the sword, it would not alter his sentiment or proceeding for American Liberty."

Three of the other Virginia delegates, Edmond Pendleton, Patrick Henry, and George Washington, did not arrive until Sunday, September 4, the day before Congress was set to open. Though Adams was silent on their arrival, Deane recorded, "[Pendleton was] of easy and cheerful countenance, polite in address, and elegant if not eloquent in style and elocution." Patrick Henry was the "the compleatest speaker" he had ever heard. Washington was a tall man of a "hard" countenance, "yet with a very young look, and an easy, soldier like air and gesture…speaks very modestly and in determined style and accent." Washington had gained notoriety for his speech in the House of Burgesses where he made the claim that he would fund, out of his own pocket, an army of 1,000 men and march them to Boston to counter the British. Washington was apprehensive about the British and the work of the Congress, writing to a friend before he left Virginia, "The crisis is arrived when we must assert our right." Otherwise, he warned, the British "shall make us tame and abject slaves, as the blacks we rule over with such arbitrary sway."

Chapter 3 - The First Continental Congress Begins

"It does not take a majority to prevail... but rather an irate, tireless minority, keen on setting brushfires of freedom in the minds of men." – Samuel Adams

The meeting of the First Continental Congress opened on Monday, September 5, 1774, at Carpenter's Hall in Philadelphia. The first order of business of the Congress was to choose a president, for which **Peyton Randolph** from Virginia was unanimously chosen. Next, **Charles Thomson** of Philadelphia was also unanimously chosen as the secretary of the Congress. The presidency of the Congress was intended as an honorary, non-executive office with the duties of chairman. Randolph, the cousin of Thomas Jefferson, was a 53-year-old London educated lawyer who had recently been speaker of the Virginia House of Burgesses. According to Silas Deane, Randolph "…seems designed by nature for business. Of an affable, open and majestic deportment—large in size, though not out of proportion, he commands respect and esteem by his very aspect, independent of the high character he sustains." The new secretary, Charles Thomson, was a hardened patriot, known as the "Sam Adams of Philadelphia." Thomson had started his life in America as a ten-year-old orphan from Ireland who had worked his way up to become the headmaster of a school and then a prosperous merchant. Thomson would serve as secretary of Congress up until the formation of the United States of America in 1789, witnessing firsthand the birth of a new nation.

Figure – Carpenter's Hall as it appears today.

Each of the delegates from their colonies had brought with them a letter with their credentials and a statement of guidance from the colonial assembly they represented. The letter was simply a note from the clerk, president, or secretary of the colonial assembly listing the names of their delegates and instructions given to them expressing their colony's wishes for the Congress. Each of the credential letters was read aloud to the Congress. The reading of the credentials of several delegations was a reminder that the purpose of the Congress was not revolution; rather, it was the redress of grievances and the restoration of harmony with Great Britain.

Massachusetts, the epicenter of the controversy, instructed her delegates:

> "…to consult upon the present state of the Colonies, and the miseries to which they are and must be reduced by the operation of certain acts of parliament respecting America, and to deliberate and determine upon wise and proper measures, to be by them recommended to all the Colonies, for the recovery and establishment of their just rights and liberties, civil and religious, and the restoration of union and harmony between Great Britain and the Colonies, most ardently desired by all good men…"

Once the credentials were read, the question became how to vote on the issues before the Congress. The larger colonies argued that it was unfair that a small colony like Rhode Island or Connecticut be given the same number of votes as a large colony like Virginia. After the delegates realized it would be complicated and a hopeless process to base votes on the population of colonies, which would have been just a wild guess at that point, they decided that each colony would get one vote. The following day the Congress took up the question again and decided on one colony, one vote.

News from Boston and an Opening Prayer

Before adornment of the second day, disturbing news arrived that the redcoats had bombarded and burnt Boston. John Adams wrote in his diary that night, "…confused account but an alarming one indeed…God grant that it may not be found true." The next day further news arrived confirming the rumored attack on Boston. "An express arrived from N. York," wrote Silas Deane to his wife, "confirming the acct. of a rupture at Boston. All is in confusion. I cannot say that all faces gather paleness, but they all gather indignation, and every tongue pronounces revenge." The news from Boston gave credence to the more radical element within Congress that sought a more reactionary response to the actions of the British.

Before the session closed on Tuesday, the delegates discussed having a prayer on Wednesday morning to open the session. One of the points of contingency with this idea was the number of diverse faiths represented in the room, leading to the question of what kind of minister should give the prayer? The group was a mix of faiths, with members from the Episcopalians, Congregationalists, Presbyterians, Quakers, and Anabaptist denominations. Samuel Adams, a pious man though given to revolutionary fervor, rose and addressed the delegates, stating he was "no bigot"; he "could hear a prayer from a gentleman of piety and virtue, who was at the same time a friend to his country." Adams moved that Reverend Mr. Duche, an Episcopalian clergyman, be requested to open Congress the next day with a prayer.

That Wednesday morning the delegates were in a state of dismay and confusion over the news, or maybe it was just an ill rumor, of the tumult in Boston. It was in that charged atmosphere that the good reverend addressed the men that September morning. He opened with a reading from the 53rd Psalm: "Plead my cause, O Lord, with them that strive with me; fight against them that fight against me. Take hold of shield and buckler and stand up for mine help. Draw out also the spear, and stop the way against them that persecute me: say unto my soul, I am thy salvation..." After the reading, Reverend Duche proceeded with an eloquent prayer. "I never," wrote John Adams on the impact of the prayer on the delegates, "saw a greater effect upon an audience. It seemed as if Heaven had ordained that psalm to be read on that morning." Silas Deane recorded his impression of the prayer: "[The reverend] prayed without book about ten minutes so pertinently, with such fervency, purity and sublimity of style and sentiment, and with such an apparent sensibility of the scenes and business before us, that even Quakers shed tears."

Figure – Opening prayer of the First Continental Congress.

The news of the bombardment of Boston turned out to be false. All that had happened was General Gage had begun to fortify the city, causing fear among the citizens. Though no blood was spilt, the rumor did serve to elevate the mood of the Congress. It was in this rarified setting that Congress set to work, appointing two committees. The first one was to prepare a statement of rights of the colonies, detail the infringements on their rights, and determine the path to restore those rights. The second committee was tasked with reporting on the statutes that affected the trade and manufacturers of the colonies.

The Suffolk Resolves

On September 16, the courier Paul Revere arrived from Boston with a copy of the Suffolk Resolves. With a ban on public meetings in Boston, delegates from Suffolk County, Massachusetts, which includes Boston, met in private homes in early September to plan resistance to the Coercive Acts. A committee headed by the patriot leader Dr. Joseph Warren was charged with drawing up an address to Governor Thomas Gage and resolves to be sent to the Continental Congress. The document listed 19 articles that detailed "infractions of the rights to which we are justly entitled by the laws of nature, the British constitution, and the charter of the providence." The five key points of the Resolves were: (1) They declared the Coercive Acts to be unconstitutional and not to be obeyed; (2) Since the British had dissolved the Massachusetts assembly, Massachusetts should create a new assembly, collect all taxes, and withhold them from the Crown until the Massachusetts government is restored; (3) The colonists should arm themselves and form their own militias in preparation for a possible British attack; (4) The jailing of any patriot leader by the British gave the colonists in turn the right to jail British officials; and (5) The document also recommended stringent economic sanctions against the British. Though the Resolves were bold in their statements against the British, the authors professed loyalty to the king and did not threaten independence. The day after the Suffolk Resolves arrived, Samuel Adams reported back to the patriots in Boston that they were "read with great applause" before the Congress.

Years later when Joseph Galloway had become a loyalist and moved to England, he wrote in a pamphlet that he believed the Suffolk Resolves were dangerous and the whole affair was orchestrated by Samuel Adams: "Mr. Adams advised and directed to be done; and when done, it was dispatched by express to Congress. By one of these expresses came the inflammatory resolves of the county of Suffolk, which contained a complete declaration of war against Great Britain." The Suffolk Resolves were applauded by some in the Congress; however, the defiant language of the document made many of the delegates extremely nervous. Action on the resolves would have to wait as the Congress now turned its attention to the delegate from Pennsylvania, Joseph Galloway, who had a proposal on how to deal with Great Britain and the Intolerable Acts.

Figure – Mural from the U.S. Capitol building. The left painting shows a colonist paying taxes. The center painting shows debate among the delegates during the First Continental Congress. The right painting shows a British solider blocking the path of a woman and child, symbolizing British oppression.

Galloway's Plan of Union

The more radical element of the delegates led by the New Englanders was opposed primarily by the Pennsylvania delegate Joseph Galloway and other sympathetic delegates. Galloway brought before the Congress a plan to change the basis of the relationship between the colonies and Great Britain. His "A Plan of a proposed Union between Great Britain and the Colonies" was to form a separate American Legislature, called the Grand Council, that would be elected by colonial assemblies. He proposed that the individual colonies continue to govern their own internal affairs with the Grand Council regulating commercial, civil, and criminal matters that affected the colonies as a whole. The Grand Council would have the authority to veto parliamentary legislation but would still be inferior to Parliament. Effectively, the Grand Council would be an inferior branch of the British Parliament. In addition to the Grand Council, his plan called for a President General appointed by the king, to administer the government.

Galloway's plan received a mixed review. It was strikingly similar to the Albany Plan, a proposal made by Benjamin Franklin at the 1754 Albany Conference. John Jay and James Duane of New York supported the plan as did Edward Rutledge of South Carolina and others. The plan was probably doomed from the start since the delegates were not empowered by their assemblies to establish a new form of government. Additionally, the plan would have impeded the rights of the colonial legislatures. The Congress voted on Galloway's Plan for Union and it was narrowly defeated in a vote of five to six. Galloway blamed what he called "the violent party" for his loss. Per the agreement of the delegates, only items that were successfully voted upon were included in the *Journals of the American Congress*. Since the Galloway Plan was not in the *Journal*, details of the plan, discussions, and debates have come down through history by personal notes kept by the delegates, of whom John Adams was the most prolific.

With the defeat of Galloway's proposal, Congress began mulling over the Suffolk Resolves once again. They realized they had not gone far enough in supporting the cause of the beleaguered colonists from Massachusetts. On Saturday, October 8, the delegates voted in a show of support for Massachusetts as recorded in the *Journals of the American Congress*: "Resolved, That this Congress approve of the opposition by the Inhabitants of the Massachusetts-Bay, to the execution of the late acts of Parliament; and if the same shall be attempted to be carried into execution by force, in such case, all America ought to support them in their opposition." Congress ordered that their resolution approving the Suffolk Resolves, along with the Resolves themselves, be printed for distribution. A further resolution was included that the colonies continue their contributions "for supplying the necessities, and alleviating distresses of our brethren at Boston."

Declaration and Resolves

One of the goals of the Continental Congress was to write a clear statement of the rights of the colonists. The process was not as straightforward as it would initially appear. Never had a Western colony taken up the path of revolution in quite this manner, leaving no historical precedence as a guide. The 13 colonies were quite different places with a wide spectrum of peoples and needs. In the New England colonies, small family farms and towns were the norm, the soil was generally rocky, slavery was of a limited nature, and the British were beginning to aggressively oppress the people. In the Southern colonies, large agricultural plantations growing tobacco, rice, cotton, and indigo dominated the society. The plantations relied upon the labor of hundreds of African slaves and indentured servants from Europe to function. The Southern colonies tended to be more closely aligned with the British Crown. This great diversity within the colonies made writing a clear statement of colonial rights a challenge.

The committee that drafted the Declaration and Resolves based their statement of rights on the laws of nature, principles of the English Constitution, and the charters of the colonies. The section begins with, "That the inhabitants of the English colonies in North-America, by the immutable laws of nature, the principles of the English constitution, and the several charters or compacts, have the following RIGHTS: Resolved, N.C.D.1. That they are entitled to life, liberty, and property, and they have never ceded to any sovereign power whatever, a right to dispose of either without their consent." Additional resolves followed that listed basic rights that were due them, including: their right of assembly, right of petition, right of trial by a jury of their peers, the right to be free of a standing army, and the right to choose their own assemblies—all rights that were basic rights defined in the English Constitution.

One of the questions that vexed the committee responsible for drafting the Declaration and Resolves was the limitations of the power of Parliament—exactly how much authority did they have over colonies? John Adams, who was on the committee, wrote, "Indeed the essence of the whole controversy; some were for a flat denial of all authority; others for denying the power of taxation only; some for denying internal, but admitting external, taxation." In the end the small committee completed their task, creating a list of colonial objections to the Intolerable Acts, a list of colonial rights, and an enumeration of their grievances with the mother country.

A Petition to King George III

Congress decided it would be wise to present their case to the other British North American colonies not present—Quebec, St. John's in Nova Scotia, Georgia, and East and West Florida. The letters explained the crisis with the British Parliament, encouraging each of them as fellow English colonists to join with the American colonies. The addresses were all prepared, reviewed by the members of Congress, and dispatched to the various colonial assemblies who had not sent delegates to the Congress. Ultimately, only Georgia would join with the struggling 12 American colonies in seeking their independence.

In addition, Congress drafted a petition to King George III informing him of the evil plot in Parliament to subvert the rights of the colonists and ensuring the king that with the successful repeal of the Coercive Acts, the colonies would restore friendly relations with Britain. The Congress appointed a committee consisting of

Richard Henry Lee, John Adams, Thomas Johnson, Patrick Henry, and John Rutledge to prepare the address to the king. The committee chose the gifted orator Patrick Henry to prepare the draft. Henry turned out to be a much better speaker than writer, forcing Congress to demand a rewrite. John Dickinson, who had joined Congress very late, was known for his writing skills so was given the task of preparing the petition. The petition listed a number of grievances against the Parliament and asked for a repeal of the Coercive Acts. By directly petitioning the king rather than Parliament, the delegates believed that the king was still the figurehead to be reckoned with to resolve their problems. Benjamin Franklin, who was in London as a colonial representative, delivered the petition to the Houses of Parliament. It wasn't until mid-January 1775 that the petition was presented to Parliament, who paid little attention to the document. Likewise, the king never responded to the Congress with a reply.

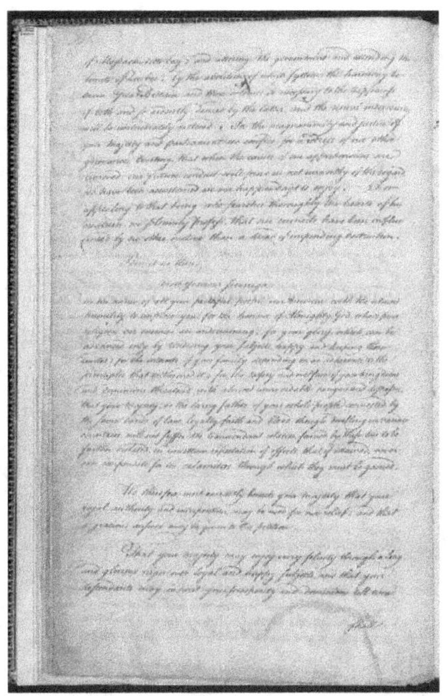

Figure – First page of the petition sent to King George III by the First Continental Congress.

Chapter 4 - Formation of the Continental Association

"Liberty, when it begins to take root, is a plant of rapid growth." – George Washington

After Congress recessed for the day, usually around three in the afternoon, the delegates went their separate ways; to work on committee assignments, explore the city, write home to their assemblies or families, or enjoy the hospitality provided by the prominent families of the city. Silas Deane wrote to his wife in mid-September telling her of a lavish dinner at the State House and of his daily routine, writing, "…Plenty of everything eatable and drinkable, and no scarcity of good humor and diversion…You will begin to suspect we do nothing else, but I assure you it is hard work. We meet at nine and sit until three, by which time we are unable to do anything but eat and drink the rest of the day." John Adams recounted his routine in Philadelphia to his wife: "My time is totally filled from the moment I get out of bed until I return to it. Visits, ceremonies, company, business, newspapers, pamphlets, etc., etc., etc." From nine to three "most earnestly engaged in debates upon the most abstruse mysteries of state"; at four a dinner "with some of the nobles of Pennsylvania," where we would "feast upon ten thousand delicacies and sit drinking Madeira, Claret, and Burgundy, till six or seven, and then go home fatigued to death..." He also detailed one of the lavish dinners he attended, describing the feast of "turtle, and every other thing, flummery, jellies, sweetmeats of twenty sorts, trifles, whipped sillabubs, floating islands, fools, etc., and then a dessert of fruits, raisins, almonds, pears, peaches. Wine most excellent and admirable. I drank Madeira at a great rate, and found no inconvenience in it."

The Continental Association

Out of the Congress came what would turn out to be one of the group's most important accomplishments, the formation of the Continental Association, or the "Association." The Association was a system that brought all the colonies into a network to enforce non-importation—the term boycott did not yet exist—of British goods. The articles of the Continental Association imposed a ban that began on December 1, 1774, on all goods from Britain, Ireland, and the British West Indies. As stated in the opening paragraphs of the articles of the Association: "To obtain redress of these Grievances, which threaten destruction to the Lives, Liberty, and Property of his Majesty's subjects in North America, we are of opinion that a Non-Importation, Non-Consumption, and Non-Exportation Agreement, faithfully adhered to, will prove the most speedy, effectual, and peaceable measure..." Since the 13 colonies were Britain's largest trading partner, a boycott of British goods would clearly get their attention.

The debate over the non-exportation provision in the Association nearly caused a rupture of Congress. Article four of the Association document stated:

> "4. The earnest desire we have not to injure our fellow-subjects in Great Britain, Ireland, or the West-Indies, induces us to suspend a non-exportation until the tenth day of September 1775; at which time, if the said acts and parts of acts of the British parliament herein after mentioned, are not repealed, we will not directly or indirectly, export any merchandise or commodity whatsoever to Great-Britain, Ireland, or the West-Indies, except rice to Europe."

The last four words, "except rice to Europe," nearly brought the Congress to an abrupt end. Four of the delegates from South Carolina, Thomas Lynch, Henry Middleton, Edward Rutledge, and John Rutledge, laid down an ultimatum that, unless the South Carolina staples of rice and indigo were exempted from the non-exportation language they would not sign the Association. To prevent a breakup of the union, a compromise was reached with the South Carolinians which allowed the non-exportation of indigo but did allow the export of rice to Europe. The crisis passed, and the delegates continued to work out the language of the Association agreement.

One of the articles in the Association's charter established committees with the colonies to enforce the non-importation, and stated: "That a committee be chosen in every County, City, and Town, by those who are qualified to vote for Representatives in the Legislature, whose business it shall be attentively to observe the conduct of all persons touching this Association; and when it shall be made to appear to the satisfaction of a majority of any such Committee, that any person with the limits of their appointment violated this Association…universally condemned as enemies of American Liberty; and thenceforth we respectively will break off all dealing with him or her." These were very contentious words for the average colonist, effectively telling them they either comply with the directives of their local Committees or become "enemies of American Liberty." The formation of the local committees to enforce the edicts of the Congress brought thousands of common people into the cause and formed a network of like-minded individuals in the colonies. Not everybody was happy with the many limitations placed on the colonists by the Association; one such person aggrieved by the new edicts complained, "If I must be enslaved, let it be by a king at least, and not by a parcel of lawless Committee-men. If I must be devoured, let me be devoured by the jaws of a lion, and not gnawed to death by rats and vermin."

After the articles of the Continental Association were finalized and approved by Congress, the delegates signed the final document, and 120 copies were ordered to be printed and distributed to the colonies. The Association was an important step toward the creation of an organic union among the colonies. Though not at the level of the Articles of Confederation or the Constitution that would follow years later, it was in a true sense an instrument of union and the first to be subscribed to by all the colonies that entered into the agreement.

The End of the First Continental Congress

At the end of October, after just seven weeks of discussion the work of this group of distinguished men came to a close. One of the final acts of the Congress was to agree to meet again in May 1775 if their grievances were not addressed. Since the petition to the king and work of the Congress would take at least six weeks to reach London, May 1775 would be enough time for the British to respond. Now the delegates dispersed back to their own colonies to deliver the messages from the Congress to the colonial assemblies. Ever the faithful diarist, John Adams recorded in his diary a hopeful note about his time in Philadelphia: "Took our departure, in a very great rain, from the happy, the peaceful, the elegant, the hospitable, and polite city of Philadelphia. It is not likely that I shall ever see this part of the world again, but I shall ever retain a most grateful, pleasing sense of the many civilities I have received in it, and shall think myself happy to have an opportunity of returning them." Oh, how very wrong Mr. Adams would prove to be regarding his belief that he would never return to "this part of the world again," for in just a few short months he would return to Philadelphia with a world of troubles upon his shoulders.

All the assemblies from the colonies, except New York and Georgia, adopted the Association. Even in these two reluctant colonies, local committees formed and went about the business of the Association with only the sanction of the general Congress.

Chapter 5 -
Aftermath of the Congress

"Timid men prefer the calm of despotism to the tempestuous sea of liberty." – Thomas Jefferson

In late 1774, the implications of the Continental Association agreement were starting to be felt within the colonies. The Committees of Inspection that were responsible for the enforcement of the non-importation mandate of the Congress became effective in carrying out the inspection for imported British goods. In New York in 1774 they imported roughly £370,000 of goods from Britain; in 1775 that number had dropped dramatically to £1,000. As the British continued to bring more troops into the Boston area, tensions between the colonists and the redcoats escalated. The colonials who were loyal to the Crown, known as "the king's friends" or "friends of the government," found it increasingly hard to remain neutral. Those loyal to Britain were viewed with suspicion and were ostracized by the rebels and patriots. The forced inspections of purchases dictated by the Continental Association irritated many, claiming the fight for American liberty was curbing the liberties of individuals. One loyalist wrote that the only liberty the patriots sought was "of knocking out any man's Brains that dares presume to speak his mind freely upon the present Contest." Choosing to remain loyal to the British Crown in the middle of a growing resistance movement had its consequences; it put your livelihood, property, and sometimes your personal safety at jeopardy. As people were forced to choose sides, friendships ended and families were torn apart.

The English Response

As word reached Britain of the entreaties of the Continental Congress and their boycott of British goods, members of Parliament and King George III became more determined to break the backs of the rebels in America. "The New England governments," proclaimed the king, "are now in a state of rebellion; blows must decide whether they are to be subject to this country or independent." More British troops were sent to North America to squash the nascent rebellion before it got out of hand. In February 1775, Parliament declared that Massachusetts was in a state of rebellion and it endorsed the king's intentions to take "the most effectual measures to enforce due obedience to the laws and authority of the Supreme Legislature." In addition, Parliament denied the New Englanders access to the North Atlantic fisheries and restricted trade outside the colonies. Later Parliament imposed the same sanctions on Pennsylvania, New Jersey, Maryland, Virginia, and South Carolina, which were considered to be supporters of Massachusetts and the Continental Congress.

As the fear of an impending war swept the colonies, people began to prepare for this grim inevitability. In Virginia, the eloquent Patrick Henry delivered a prophetic speech to his fellow Burgesses, "The next gale from the north will bring to ears the clash of resounding arms." Though the exact words of his speech were not recorded, his closing statement, "Give me liberty or give me death!" became the rallying cry of the revolutionaries. On the fateful morning of April 19, 1775, on Lexington Green in Massachusetts, a small band of colonial Minutemen, mainly farmers and their sons, faced off against hundreds of British regulars. Shots were fired, lives were lost, and an eight-year struggle for the independence of the American colonies against the most powerful army in the world had begun.

The End

Thank you for purchasing this book. I hope you enjoyed reading it. Please don't forget to leave a review of the book. I read each one and they help me become a better writer.

-Doug

Timeline of the First Continental Congress

May 1773 – Parliament passes the Tea Act, which grants the British East India Company a monopoly on tea sales in British America.

December 16, 1773 – About 160 patriots disguised as Mohawk Indians dump over 300 chests of British tea into Massachusetts Bay. The event becomes known as the Boston Tea Party.

March 31, 1774 – Parliament passes a series of laws called the Coercive Acts, known as the Intolerable Acts in the American colonies, that are designed to punish the colony of Massachusetts Bay for the Boston Tea Party.

May 3, 1774 – British General Thomas Gage arrives in Boston to establish military control of the city.

Mid-June 1774 – Additional British troops begin landing in Boston.

September 3, 1774 – General Gage begins fortifying Boston.

September 5, 1774 – First day of the First Continental Congress meets at Carpenter's Hall in Philadelphia, Pennsylvania.

September 17, 1774 – Congress endorses the Suffolk Resolves.

October 8, 1774 - Congress votes to "approve the opposition of the inhabitants of the Massachusetts-Bay, to the execution of the late acts of Parliament…"

October 14, 1774 – Congress adopts the Declaration of Colonial Rights.

October 20, 1774 – Congress forms the Continental Association, which signifies increased cooperation among the colonies.

October 22, 1774 – Galloway's Plan of Union is defeated in Congress by a vote of six to five. Henry Middleton voted in as the new president of Congress due to Peyton Randolph's serious illness.

October 26, 1774 – Last day of the First Continental Congress. Congress approves the Petition to King George III. The Massachusetts Provisional Congress organizes the "Minutemen" within their militia.

April 19, 1775 – The first military engagements of the Revolutionary War occur between regular British troops and colonial militia at Lexington and Concord, Massachusetts.

Biographical Sketches

<u>Adams, John</u> (1735 – 1826) was an American statesman and Founding Father who served as the first vice president and second president of the United States. John Adams was born in Braintree, Massachusetts, to parents of modest means, graduated from Harvard College in 1755, studied law, and became a successful lawyer in Boston. Adams was a delegate from Massachusetts to the Continental Congress, where he played an important role in persuading Congress to declare independence. He assisted Thomas Jefferson in writing the Declaration of Independence in 1776 and was its foremost advocate in the Congress. As a diplomat in Europe, he helped negotiate the eventual peace treaty with Great Britain and acquired vital governmental loans from Amsterdam bankers. Adams was the primary author of the Massachusetts Constitution in 1780 and influenced the development of America's own Constitution. After serving as the American minister to Great Britain and as vice president under George Washington, Adams was elected as president in 1796. Much of his term as president was consumed with the so-called Quasi-War with France, an undeclared naval war arising from the general European conflict spawned by the French Revolution. Adams' unpopular policies, plus his long-standing feud with Alexander Hamilton, divided the Federalist party, which contributed to his defeat in the presidential election of 1800 to Thomas Jefferson. After

the presidency, Adams retired to his farm in Braintree, writing his memoirs, essays on his wartime diplomacy, and political theory.

Figure – John Adams.

Adams, Samuel (1722 – 1803) was an American radical political agitator during the Revolutionary Era of America and one of the Founding Fathers of the United States. Samuel Adams was a native of Boston and was educated at Harvard. After several attempts at his own business, he worked as a tax collector and for the Massachusetts legislature as a clerk. Adams was a noted polemicist and popular leader against the Stamp Act and the Townshend Duties. He was a ringleader in the Sons of Liberty and helped organize the Boston Tea Party in 1773. Adams was a delegate from Massachusetts to the First Continental Congress where he supported the radical Suffolk Resolves. He was a member of the Second Continental Congress from 1775 to 1781 where he was a signer of the Declaration of Independence. Later in his life he was the lieutenant governor and then governor of Massachusetts. Samuel Adams was a preeminent early leader in America's quest for freedom from Britain. Thomas Jefferson said he was "truly the Man of the revolution."

Figure – Samuel Adams.

<u>Dickinson, John</u> (1732 – 1808) was a Founding Father of the United States of America, known as the "Penman of the Revolution." John Dickinson was born in Maryland, then moved to Delaware as a young boy. He was educated by tutors at home until he studied law under John Moland in Philadelphia. Next, he studied law in London for three years, retuning to Philadelphia to practice law. He soon entered politics as a member of the Pennsylvania legislature where he was a staunch conservative, an ideology he would hold for the rest of his life. As the British became more aggressive with new laws and taxes on the American colonies, Dickinson began writing articles and pamphlets on the growing crisis. He is most remembered for a series of articles he published anonymously titled, *Letters from a Farmer in Pennsylvania to the Inhabitants of the British Colonies.* Dickinson was active in the American revolutionary cause, serving as chairman of the Philadelphia Committee of Correspondence, as a delegate to the First and Second Continental Congress. He gained a negative notoriety as being one of only a handful of delegates in the Second Continental Congress who did not sign the Declaration of Independence out of a belief that the colonies should not separate from Great Britain. He left the Congress shortly after not signing the declaration and joined the Continental Army. After the war, Dickinson took part in the 1787 Constitutional Convention and helped draft the nation's new Constitution. He published a series of letters under the pen name "Fabius" strongly urging the ratification of the Constitution by the states.

Figure – John Dickinson.

<u>Galloway, Joseph</u> (1731 – 1803) was an American politician during the Revolutionary Era, who served in both the Pennsylvania Provincial Assembly and the First Continental Congress. Born in Maryland, Joseph Galloway moved with his father to Philadelphia in 1749 where he received his education. He became a lawyer and then a member of the Pennsylvania Provincial Assembly from 1756 to 1774. In 1776, he was a member of the Pennsylvania delegation to the First Continental Congress. In Congress, he represented the conservative faction and is most known for his Plan of Union, which proposed that colonists form their own parliament subject to the Crown. During the Revolutionary War he joined with the British and assisted them during the occupation of Philadelphia. In 1778, he fled to Britain along with his daughter. His estates in America were

confiscated by the colonial government and he was forced to live off his British pension. He never returned to America, living in exile in Britain until his death.

Figure – Joseph Galloway.

King George III (1738 – 1820) was the king of Great Britain and Ireland from 1760 until his death in 1820. George III, whose given name was George William Frederick, ascended to the throne of Great Britain and Ireland at age 22 upon the death of his grandfather, George II. He became king during the French and Indian War or the Seven Years' War as it was called in Europe, in which Britain defeated the French and drove them out of what is now the United States. The year after ascending to the throne, he married the German Princess Charlotte of Mecklenburg-Strelitz, whom he met on the day of their wedding. King George took a hardline approach to the rebellious colonies in America, which led to a protracted and expensive war with the colonies. After the defeat of the British in the American Revolutionary War, Britain was once again at war with France during the Napoleon Wars. In his later years, the king's recurrent mental illness became permanent. It is believed that his illness was due to a bipolar disorder or the blood disease porphyria. In 1810, his eldest son, George, Prince of Wales, ruled Great Britain as Prince Regent until his father's death.

Figure – King George III.

Randolph, Peyton (1721 – 1775) was the attorney general of Virginia, speaker of the House of Burgesses, and first president of the Continental Congress. Peyton Randolph was born into a prominent Virginia family, educated at the College of William and Mary, and then in London. He became a lawyer at Williamsburg and was appointed King's Attorney (attorney general) for the province. Randolph was a member of the Virginia House of Burgesses for several terms. He was named as one of the seven delegates to the First Continental Congress in 1774 and in turn was elected the president of the Congress. He suffered from poor health and had to resign before the end of the first Congress. Thomas Jefferson wrote of him: "He was indeed a most excellent man; and none was ever more beloved and respected by his friends. Somewhat cold and coy towards strangers, but of the sweetest affability when ripened into acquaintance."

Figure – Peyton Randolph.

<u>Thomson, Charles</u> (1729 – 1824) was the secretary of the Continental Congress from 1774 to 1789. He was born in Ireland and emigrated to America at age ten. Charles Thomson arrived in America with his siblings as orphans, as his mother had died in Ireland and his father died aboard ship during their journey to America. He was taken in and received a good education. After being the headmaster of a Latin school, he turned his attention to the mercantile trade. During the American Revolutionary period, Thomson became active in the patriot cause for independence from Great Britain. John Adams wrote of him, "the Sam Adams of Philadelphia, the life of the cause of liberty, they say." Thomson became the secretary of the First Continental Congress in 1774 and retained the post until George Washington became president of the United States in 1789. In retirement, he translated the Greek Septuagint and the New Testament to produce the 1808 four-volume set of Thomson's *The Holy Bible, Containing the Old and New Covenant, Commonly Called the Old and New Testament.*

Figure – Charles Thomson.

References and Further Readings

Boyer, Paul S. (Editor in Chief) *The Oxford Companion to United States History*. Oxford: Oxford University Press, 2001.

Burnett, Edmund Cody. *The Continental Congress*. New York: Macmillan Company, 1941.

Dictionary of American Biography. New York: Charles Scribner's Sons, 1928-1995.

Kutler, Stanley I. (Editor in Chief). *Dictionary of American History*. Third Edition. New York: Thomson Gale, 2003.

McCullough, David. *John Adams*. New York: Simon & Schuster, 2002.

Montross, Lynn. *The Reluctant Rebels: The Story of the Continental Congress 1774-1790*. New York: Harper & Brothers Publishing, 1950.

Norton, Mary Beth. *1774 The Long Year of Revolution*. New York: Vintage Books, 2020.

Randall, Willard S. *George Washington: A Life*. New York: Owl Books, *1997*.

The Encyclopedia Americana, International Edition. New York: Americana Corporation, 1968.

Tindall, George B. and David E. Shi. *America: A Narrative History*. Seventh Edition. New York: W.W. Norton & Company, 2007.

West, Doug. *Samuel Adams: A Short Biography: Architect of the American Revolution*. Missouri: C&D Publications, 2019.

Wood, Gordon S. *The American Revolution: A History*. New York: The Modern Library, 2003.

Acknowledgements

I would like to thank Cynthia West and Lisa Zahn for their help in preparation of this book. All the photographs are from the public domain. The quotes at the beginning of each chapter are from Brainyquotes.com.

About the Author

Doug West is a retired engineer, small business owner, and experienced writer with several books to his credit. His writing interests are general, with expertise in science, history, and biographies. Doug has a B.S. in Physics from the Missouri School of Science and Technology and a Ph.D. in General Engineering from Oklahoma State University. He lives with his wife and little dog "Millie" near Kansas City, Missouri. Additional books by Doug West can be found at https://www.amazon.com/Doug-West/e/B00961PJ8M. Follow the author on Facebook at:
https://www.facebook.com/30minutebooks.

Figure – Doug West (photo by Karina West)

Additional Books in
the 30 Minute Book Series

All books are by Doug West unless otherwise noted.

A Short Biography of the Scientist Sir Isaac Newton

A Short Biography of the Astronomer Edwin Hubble

Galileo Galilei – A Short Biography

Benjamin Franklin – A Short Biography

The American Revolutionary War – A Short History

The Astronomer Cecilia Payne-Gaposchkin – A Short Biography

Dr. Walter Reed – A Short Biography by Erin Delong

Coinage of the United States – A Short History

John Adams – A Short Biography

Alexander Hamilton – A Short Biography

The Great Depression – A Short History

Jesse Owens, Adolf Hitler and the 1936 Summer Olympics

Thomas Jefferson – A Short Biography

The French and Indian War – A Short History

The Mathematician John Forbes Nash Jr. – A Short Biography

Vice President Mike Pence – A Short Biography

President Jimmy Carter – A Short Biography

Ernest Rutherford: A Short Biography: The Father of Nuclear Physics

Sir William Crookes: A Short Biography: Nineteenth-Century British Chemist and Spiritualist

The Journey of Apollo 11 to the Moon

William Henry Harrison: A Short Biography: Tenth President of the United States

John Tyler: A Short Biography: Eleventh President of the United States

James K. Polk: A Short Biography: Eleventh President of the United States

Samuel Adams: A Short Biography: Architect of the American Revolution

The Mexican-American War: A Short History: America's Fulfillment of Manifest Destiny

History of the Plymouth and Massachusetts Bay Colonies: Pilgrims, Puritans, and the Founding of New England

The History of the Jamestown Colony: America's First Permanent English Settlement

Zachary Taylor: A Short Biography: Twelfth President of the United States

Herbert Hoover: A Short Biography: Thirty-First President of the United States

The Great 1929 Stock Market Crash: A Short History

Christopher Columbus and the Discovery of the Americas

The Formation of the 13 Colonies in America: A Short History

Religion in Colonial America: A Short History

George Washington: A Short Biography: First President of the United States

Dr. Benjamin Rush: A Short Biography: Physician and Founding Father of America

The 1918 Spanish Flu Pandemic in America: A Short History

The Ancient Milesian Philosophers: Thales, Anaximander, Anaximenes: A Short Introduction to Their Lives and Works

Martha Washington: First Lady of the United States: A Short Biography

Index